Original title:
A Love So Strong

Copyright © 2024 Creative Arts Management OÜ
All rights reserved.

Author: James Anderson
ISBN HARDBACK: 978-9916-94-718-0
ISBN PAPERBACK: 978-9916-94-719-7

When Stars Align

In a galaxy so bright, we twirl,
My socks don't match, but hey, they swirl!
Your laughter's like a cosmic plan,
Together we dance, you're my biggest fan.

Under moonlit skies, we play charades,
Your funny faces never fade.
Jumping on meteors, we soar and glide,
With you here, I'm a goofy bride.

Whispered Promises

You whispered sweet nothings in my ear,
Like ice cream dreams, and wash away fear.
Promises made in candy-coated tones,
In this love fest, we're all sticks and cones.

Pinky-swears under a starlit tree,
You're my partner in silly, can't you see?
We'll write our vows on silly putty,
With a grin so wide, our hearts feel nutty.

Infinite Embrace

Our hugs are like a trampoline's bounce,
You giggle so much, I'd swear you'd pounce.
Infinite snuggles, a comical plight,
In the quilt of our laughter, we sleep at night.

When we cook, oh, what a sight,
Flour fights and veggies in flight.
In this oversized warmth, we cocoon,
You're my silly star under a winking moon.

Heartstrings Entwined

Our heartstrings twang like a rubber band,
Together we form the silliest band.
You play the spoons, I bang on a pot,
In this symphony of chaos, we're hot!

With each goofy joke, our bond grows tight,
Like two puzzle pieces, what a delight.
In a cardboard box, we dream and scheme,
Sailing through life's most whimsical dream.

Blossoms of Lasting Connection

In a garden where laughter grows,
We plant our seeds without a care,
Ticklish bees and playful crows,
Sprout blooms of joy everywhere.

With every petal, silly dance,
We twirl and spin, we grab the sun,
In this quirky happenstance,
We find our hearts, we've just begun.

Roots tangled tight, we laugh and tease,
Like vines that climb and intertwine,
A flower's giggle in the breeze,
Forever yours, and you are mine.

So here's to blossoms sprouting free,
With jams and jellies made of cheer,
In this garden, you'll always see,
Our crazy love will persevere.

Winds of Unwavering Loyalty

On a kite we fly up high,
Chasing clouds, just you and me,
In the wind, a playful sigh,
We dance with leaves, wild and free.

Whispers of a cheeky breeze,
Tickle our hearts as we explore,
With every gust, we aim to please,
Loyalty's a funny chore.

We sail through storms, with laughs to spare,
An umbrella for each rainy day,
Your goofy grin is always there,
In gusts of love, we sway and play.

So lift your hands, embrace the air,
Let's dive in wild, with no regret,
For in this dance, our hearts ensnare,
A bond that's hard to forget.

Underneath a Starlit Promise

Beneath the stars, we share a joke,
With constellations twinkling bright,
You snort and laugh, I barely choke,
As comets dance in full delight.

The moon our stage, we mime our dreams,
Silly wishes whispered low,
In the dark, our laughter beams,
Together, we put on a show.

Giggles echo through the night,
As shooting stars sweep by with grace,
Our promises, a funny sight,
In starlit vows, we find our place.

With each twinkle, we forge ahead,
In this grand cosmic ballet,
Underneath, we giggle instead,
Just you and me, come what may.

Cradle of Unending Trust

In a hammock, we swing and sway,
Giggling like children at play,
Trust wrapped up in warm embrace,
We snooze and dream, a happy space.

With every poke and gentle shove,
We tease, we laugh, we never fight,
In our cocoon, it's purest love,
Worn-out slippers and late-night bites.

Together, we build pillow forts,
As guardians of our silly reign,
In this world of goofy ports,
We trust each other just the same.

So here's our cozy little space,
Where snickers bloom and worries rust,
In this cradle, joy takes place,
Two hearts unite in endless trust.

Unyielding Togetherness

In a world of mismatched socks,
We bumble in our paradox.
Your laugh's a tickle, my clumsy fall,
Together we burst, we capture it all.

You steal my fries, I swipe your seat,
An arm wrestle ends in defeat.
With every giggle and playful shove,
We prove we're not just in love.

We dance like penguins on ice,
Tripping over our own device.
You're my partner in silly spree,
In this wild patchwork tapestry.

Through daily chaos and grand displays,
We navigate life in countless ways.
Our bond, a riot, forever robust,
In you, my friend, I put my trust.

Dance of the Souls

With two left feet, we sway and spin,
Our rhythm's a chaos born from within.
You take the lead, and I can't quite follow,
Yet here we are, never feeling hollow.

Your quirky moves make me snort,
We burst laughing, both cut short.
Like deer on ice, we twirl and leap,
Our silly dance, a treasured heap.

In tangled arms, we stumble and glide,
Each turn a burst of pure joy, a ride.
Our hearts beat a tune of peculiar charm,
With every clumsy step, you keep me warm.

As we spin through this comical dream,
Life's a stage, and we're the team.
Our dance, a symphony all our own,
In harmony, our laughter has grown.

Canvas of Two

With splatters of paint, we start our day,
You pick the color, I pick the spray.
Our walls are canvas, our hearts the hues,
In a mess of colors, we seldom lose.

Your brush strokes wild, mine steady and neat,
Creating a picture, oh-so-sweet.
A masterpiece born from chaos and play,
It's a beautiful mess in every way.

With an epic splash, I'll wear your red,
You smudge my cheek and claim it's the thread.
Each color drips with laughter and cheer,
In this lively mural, we have no fear.

When the canvas dries, our hearts will show,
A portrait of fun, our love aglow.
With every stroke, our story unfolds,
A masterpiece cherished, our joy never folds.

Symphony of Us

In a world of tunes, we found our beat,
Your off-key notes make life so sweet.
We harmonize in the funniest ways,
Crafting laughter to fill our days.

With pots for drums and spoons for strings,
We create a world where joy always sings.
Trumpets from the kitchen, a symphony grand,
Together we're goofy, hand in hand.

You play the clown, while I laugh out loud,
Our melody dances, we're lost in the crowd.
With each playful note, a smile shines through,
In this orchestra fine, it's just me and you.

As the curtains draw on this playful act,
Our love strikes a chord, a beautiful pact.
With laughter as music, our hearts stay strong,
In the symphony of life, we always belong.

Journey of the Heart

We started off with coffee stains,
And silly jokes that left us drained.
You laughed so hard, you spilled your cup,
And I just knew, we'd never give up.

Through every mishap, giggles flowed,
On our wild paths, where love has glowed.
From dancing dogs to missing keys,
With you, my dear, it's all a breeze.

Riding bikes with flatting tires,
Creating chaos, lighting fires.
You found my socks all in a heap,
Yet still, you say, I'm worth the leap.

So let's embrace this quirky ride,
With you right here, I'm filled with pride.
In every laugh and goofy scene,
Together we're the funny dream.

Merging Stars

In silly twirls beneath the night,
We danced and bumped like stars in flight.
You stepped on toes, I lost my breath,
Yet in this mess, I felt no death.

Your jokes collide with my shy gaze,
Creating laughter in a daze.
With every pun, our hearts take charge,
We merge like planets, oh so large.

Each wink you give, a cosmic spark,
Turning our fumbles into art.
You're like the moon, I'm just a comet,
Together, we have found our sonnet.

So here's to us, a stellar crew,
Twinkling brightly, just us two.
With goofy grins that never fade,
In this game of love, we've got it made.

The Language of Togetherness

With a wink and nod, we share a code,
In giggles and grins, our hearts explode.
You say 'hello' with a funny face,
In this language, love finds its place.

Through whispers soft and playful shoves,
We translate all our silly loves.
From silly puns to playful jests,
In this dialect, we are the best.

You misplaced my keys, but I don't mind,
You found them in the fridge, oh my, my kind!
Every blunder, a sweet delight,
In our unique world, everything's right.

So let's keep talking, hearts in sync,
In laughter's language, we will link.
Every chuckle a testament clear,
Together forever, my dear, my dear.

Heartfelt Horizons

Together we sail on winds of glee,
To horizons wide, we roam so free.
Your snorts and giggles fill the air,
With every wave, we toss our care.

We built a life with laughter's glue,
Creating scenes, just me and you.
From clumsy dances to kitchen fights,
Our love shines bright like neon lights.

In every blunder, a tale unfolds,
The tapestry of warmth, our hearts behold.
You tripped on air, I nearly cried,
Yet through it all, we'll never hide.

So here's to love that's silly and true,
With every burst of laughter, I choose you.
On these horizons, let's sail along,
In this journey, my heart feels strong.

The Bridge Between Souls

Each joke we share is like a thread,
Weaving laughter where we tread.
In every giggle, in every snort,
We find a bond that can't be bought.

With silly faces, we bond and tease,
Like two kids climbing up the trees.
Your quirky dance, oh what a sight!
Makes my heart feel light as flight.

In every prank, in every jest,
You bring out my very best.
Like peanut butter loves its jam,
Together we're a witty scam.

Oh, how we laugh, what a grand show,
You tickle my heart, just so you know!
In this circus of our delight,
We juggle joy with all our might.

Timeless Togetherness

You steal my fries, and I don't mind,
In every bite, sweet love we find.
Your laugh like music fills the air,
Like pop rocks bursting without a care.

We wear matching socks, a fashion blunder,
But our quirky ways keep us from thunder.
Each shared wink lights up the room,
You're the sunshine that chases gloom.

In endless memes, we find our glee,
Your silliness suits me perfectly.
Like two socks stuck in the wash,
Forever mixed, we're always posh.

In our warm bubble, we spin and twirl,
Life's a comic, and you're my pearl.
Through tickles and jokes, our hearts align,
In this funny dance, you're forever mine.

Together in the Breeze

As we chase kites on the sunny hill,
Your laughter echoes, a joyful thrill.
With cheesy puns and silly screams,
We weave our lives with playful dreams.

You trip and laugh, fall into the grass,
Rolling and giggling, wishing time would pass.
Under the sun, we sing off-key,
Happily dancing, just you and me.

With ice cream spills and messy clothes,
Our life—a fairytale, everyone knows.
Like two kids dressed in mismatched shoes,
Together we laugh, there's nothing we lose.

In the calm breeze, we find our song,
Through every storm, we just tag along.
You and I, a duo so free,
In laughter's hold, just let it be.

In the Silence We Speak

In quiet moments, we exchange a glance,
Like two old pals sharing a dance.
Your goofy smile says it all,
In this stillness, I feel so tall.

With a side-eye wink and a silly face,
You fill my world with vibrant grace.
Like secret whispers beneath the night,
Our love's a jest, yet feels so right.

We invent stories, just you and I,
Like spunky squirrels racing by.
In the silence, we find our fun,
With you, my dear, the laughter has begun.

Through quiet laughter, our hearts collide,
In cherished comfort, we find our pride.
With every chuckle, our spirits link,
In this calm, I hear you think.

Underneath the same Sky

We bump like two cars at a red light,
Both of us laughing—oh, what a sight.
Your coffee spills, and then mine too,
Guess we're just racing to start anew.

Chasing sunsets on a skateboard drawn,
With your quirky dance, I can't help but yawn.
But every wrong step gives me a cheer,
Who knew goofing around could feel so dear?

Wearing mismatched socks without a care,
You say it's fashion; I just smile and stare.
We share ice cream—no, we both dive in,
That extra scoop? Let the fun begin!

Under this sky, our laughter flows,
Life's a big joke that only we know.
No map required for this silly spree,
Just you and I—oh, let us be free!

Threads of Moonlit Dreams

We spun like tops on a moonlit street,
Your dance moves could knock anyone off their feet.
With a goofy grin, you trip and fall,
But every stumble says you've got the gall.

Making wishes on stars while we tease,
While moonlight shines, we're just swaying with ease.
You said you'd grab dinner, but charred it bright,
How can burnt toast feel so right tonight?

Crafting magic with glitter and glue,
Our sparkly mess is a sight—who knew?
Your wild ideas keep me on my toes,
Like building a rocket from cardboard—who knows?

So here we are, in our whimsical scheme,
Two dorks in a world that can only redeem.
With mischief in heart and dreams that gleam,
We weave the fabric of our silly dream!

Beyond the Seasons

We build a snowman in June's heat,
Laughing at how we can't feel our feet.
With a snowball fight that's a total flop,
But those frosty giggles? We just can't stop.

Autumn leaves dance, like us in the park,
Our funny selfies are an echoed remark.
You pretend to trip, and I swear you've flown,
Laughter echoes, like a sweet summer drone.

When flowers bloom, and the world smells sweet,
You show up in rain boots for our warm-weather feat.
Dancing through petals like a wildlife show,
Are they chasing us, or are we chasing? Who knows?

Through snowy breaths and sunshine rays,
We'll make every season one big parade.
Hand in hand, we embrace spring's fresh breeze,
Finding joy in each laugh, letting worries freeze.

Heartfelt Adventures

We're two clowns at the best of a show,
With a pie in the face as our big hello.
Your jokes crack me up—like the sound of a horn,
Life's a circus, filled with laughter since dawn.

In the park, you wear socks on your hands,
While I try to figure out if that makes you grand.
We role-play aliens from planet goo,
Who knew our missions were just barbecue?

With a map upside down, we roam the town,
Every corner holds giggles, never a frown.
From finding the lost to eating ice cream,
Every little moment turns into a dream!

So here's to the fun that never goes old,
Our adventures are silly, and worth more than gold.
With you by my side, I'll never be bored,
Just one heart and one laugh—this life can be scored!

The Strength in Us

We laugh at our quirks, how we both snore,
You steal the covers, yet I love you more.
With every misstep, we dance 'til we fall,
Together we rise, we're the champs of it all.

Our inside jokes, oh how they ignite,
You trip on my shoes, but it feels so right.
A fortress of smiles, we built brick by brick,
In this silly world, you're my favorite trick.

Chords of Connection

You strum on my heart like a guitar gone wild,
Each note adds a giggle, we're the perfect child.
With every flat tire, we just laugh and scream,
Navigating life's road, we're a crazy team.

Your laugh is a song, that I can't resist,
In the playlist of love, you top the list.
From pancakes burned black, to that dance in the rain,
Every off-key moment is never in vain.

The Journey of Us

We trip and we tumble, but oh what a ride,
With you as my partner, I'm filled with pride.
Maps may get lost, but we'll find our way,
Stumbling through life, we make every day.

With snacks on the seats, and tunes on blast,
Your jokes at red lights, oh they come so fast.
Through hiccups and giggles, our path is so bright,
Together we're silly, navigating the night.

A Promise Never Fades

With each wacky moment, our bond only grows,
Like the odd socks found, nobody knows!
You're the punchline to every goofy joke,
In the circus of life, you're my favorite bloke.

Our vows may be silly, but they're quite profound,
In this crazy adventure, we're thoroughly bound.
From pranks to sweet whispers, through all of the fray,
In this whimsical story, we'll gladly replay.

Shadows and Light Combined

In the dance of day and night,
You steal my fries, and that feels right.
With every laugh, we break the rules,
Who knew we'd act like two old fools?

Your quirks, they light up the whole room,
Like two balloons, we're destined to zoom.
In silly selfies, we make our art,
You're the peanut butter to my tart!

With pun-filled texts that fly so fast,
We share our cake, but you eat the last.
Two mismatched socks, we embrace the odd,
Like a quirky dream that's always broad!

So here's to us, a joyful spree,
With every prank, we're wild and free.
In this world of giggles, we belong,
As we tango to a funny song.

Anchored in Each Other

You're my anchor, I'm your boat,
Floating together, what a note!
In crazy storms, we ride the waves,
With laughter's might, our hearts it saves.

We bicker over who should drive,
But in this funny love, we thrive.
In pillow fights, we lose our way,
Then snuggle close at the end of the day.

Calling you names just for fun,
You grin at me, and then you run.
Our playful jabs are never mean,
A circus act, a hilarious scene!

With popcorn fights and movie nights,
We share the giggles, scaling heights.
In every pun, we find our cheer,
Anchored tightly, you are my dear.

Wings of Solidarity

Like two silly geese that can't quite fly,
We waddle together, and oh, my!
With goofy pranks that make us snort,
We hoot and holler in our own court.

You make the best spaghetti mess,
With every twirl, our laughter's excess.
In this kitchen chaos, we unite,
Stirring up love in every bite!

Under dim lights, we dance away,
With two left feet, what a display!
You step on toes, but I just grin,
In this happy chaos, we always win.

Together we flutter, like two odd birds,
Sharing our secrets and silly words.
With a wink and a nod, we take our flight,
In wings of laughter, we soar so bright!

Unfolding Like Petals

In the garden of quirks, we bloom and sway,
You crack me up in every way.
With giggles growing like petals wide,
Together in humor, we take a ride.

Your cheesy jokes are simply divine,
Like flowers lifting up on a vine.
In pollen fights, we shake and tease,
Flirting with nature, we do as we please.

As we dance in the sun's warm embrace,
Even our shadows know how to chase.
We're petal-soft but can plant our roots,
In this silly love, we bear the fruits!

With every new sprout, our laughter grows,
In the garden of life, oh how it shows!
An endless bloom, our spirits rise,
Unfolding like petals, beneath the skies.

Echoes of Affection

I once gave my heart a little nudge,
It jumped right back, said, 'No more grudge!'
We danced around like two clumsy fools,
Creating chaos, breaking all the rules.

Your laugh's a tune, a silly song,
We sing off-key and get it wrong.
Yet every smile brightens the room,
Like daisies sprouting in full bloom.

We play the fool, trip over our dreams,
Chasing sunshine, bursting at the seams.
Your goofy charm, my sweet delight,
In this grand circus, we take flight.

So here's to us, the jesters at heart,
In this comedy show, we're the best part.
Together we tangle in joy, oh dear,
With echoes of laughter that always cheer.

The Fire Within

You're like a spark from an old firecracker,
With every word, my laughter's a quacker.
We roast our marshmallows with hot, silly jokes,
Creating s'mores from our quirky folks.

At dinner dates, we juggle our fries,
You steal my ketchup, then bat your eyes.
I chase you around with a fork in hand,
Like playful pirates, we make our stand.

Our love's an ember, oh so absurd,
It's fueled by laughter, not just the word.
We dance in the kitchen like experts in glee,
Whipping up chaos, just you and me.

Through the flames, we tumble, we swirl,
A bonfire romance in this crazy whirl.
With laughter igniting each moment we live,
In this wild blaze, we both forgive.

Threads of Devotion

We're stitched together with a goofy thread,
A tapestry woven in silly instead.
Your knitting skills, oh what a sight,
From socks to sweaters, it's quite the fright!

Each loop and twist, a tale to unfold,
With every purl, our stories retold.
You tangled the yarn, now it's a mess,
But in our chaos, I must confess.

We quilt our dreams with mismatched hues,
Laughing so hard, we spill our blues.
Your fashion sense, well, it's unique,
In our patchwork hearts, we don't critique.

So here we are, a colorful pair,
With each stitch sewn, there's love in the air.
In this fabric of fun, we shall reside,
Threads of devotion, our joyful ride.

Daring to Dream Together

We're dreamers at heart, but clumsy, you see,
Trying to tango while spilling our tea.
You trip on your hopes, I leap and I sway,
In this wacky dance, we find our way.

Your ambitions soar like a cat with a plan,
I'm right behind, a juggler without a hand.
We chase after stars with a pop and a zing,
Creating a symphony, our own kind of fling.

Bouncing on rainbows, we dare to glide,
Chasing our whims, we run side by side.
With pies in the oven and dreams in the air,
We steal each moment, without a care.

So let's leap together, take the plunge,
In this joyful duet, we'll never grunge.
With each daring step, our hearts will entwine,
Laughing through life, your hand in mine.

Unyielding Affection

In the kitchen, we laugh and play,
Cooking dinner in our silly way.
You burned the toast, I dropped the fries,
Yet still, we dance with twinkling eyes.

We bake our joys, frosted with glee,
Your secret recipe, a mystery.
Through flour fights and giggles' thrill,
My heart just jumps, what more could fill?

You snore like thunder, oh what a sound,
While I tiptoe, trying not to rebound.
But every snore's a lullaby sweet,
In our little chaos, love's bittersweet.

We bicker 'bout who's the best at games,
Each playful jab, our hearts inflames.
In every jest, there's truth we share,
Together forever, a perfect pair.

The Fire That Never Fades

You steal my fries while I'm not aware,
I pretend to be mad, but you just stare.
With playful nudges, you make me laugh,
Like a clown named Chuck who's lost his path.

We argue 'bout who's the greatest chef,
But lunch at noon is our little theft.
With every burnt edge, oh what a dish,
We eat it gladly, along with wish.

You steal the covers in the dead of night,
But I won't complain, you're a funny sight.
With limbs all tangled in midnight's embrace,
Dreams unfold, filled with silly grace.

We chuckle at moments, both big and small,
In your embrace, I'm never too tall.
You're my partner, my laughter, my fit,
In this circus of life, we both admit.

Beyond Words and Time

We speak in glances, one quirky glance,
Your quirky jokes lead to happy dance.
Every time you trip over your own shoes,
The laughter echoes, it's always good news.

On our lazy days, we binge-watch shows,
Your popcorn skills? Oh, who even knows?
With butter battles and soda wars,
Our love's a comedy full of roars.

You sing off-key in the shower's space,
Yet somehow, I miss that goofy face.
Each note you hit, a hilarious quack,
In the symphony of us, there's no lack.

Through silly fights and playful tease,
We find our rhythm with the greatest ease.
In every moment, laughter's the prime,
An endless joke, beyond words and time.

Hearts Entwined in Silence

In silence, we share a mischievous grin,
As we dance round the house, oh it's a win.
The pillow fight that leads to the floor,
With giggles and squeals, we always want more.

Your secret stash of snacks is a steal,
Every hidden chip makes the day surreal.
With a wink and a nod, I keep the score,
But when you're around, I always want more.

The way we argue over the dog's bed,
Who sleeps where? It's all in my head.
Yet, every tuggle, every silly spat,
Brings us closer, just as we sat.

In quiet moments, we share a glance,
Intertwined hearts still find their dance.
With laughter that rings through the softest night,
In our sweet silence, everything feels right.

A Safe Harbor

In your arms, I find my rest,
Like socks that fit, you're simply the best.
Through storms and gales, you're my delight,
Even on days when you snore all night.

You steal my fries, that's quite a feat,
Yet somehow, it's still a treat.
You dance like a fish, unaware of the show,
But together, we laugh, and that's how we grow.

Your jokes are silly; they tickle my soul,
Like kittens in boots, you make me whole.
Through spilt drinks and burnt toast, we thrive,
In our quirky world, we feel so alive.

So here's to us, the oddest pair,
With love and laughter, beyond compare.
Let's sail the seas, without a care,
For in this harbor, we've found our lair.

Blossoms in the Night

Under the stars, your face aglow,
Like a flower shop's best, you steal the show.
We giggle at nothing, it's pure delight,
With you, silly moments feel just right.

You paint my world in vibrant hues,
With antics and pranks that chase away blues.
Your puns may confuse, yet make me grin,
Like bees on a hive, I'm drawn to your spin.

When you trip on your feet or slip on a shoe,
I can't help but laugh, because it's so you.
Our love blooms bright, it's never mundane,
Like daisies in the sun, we shine through the rain.

So let's dance in the moonlight, make memories sweet,
With blossoms that flourish, we'll never know defeat.
In this whimsical garden, our hearts intertwine,
As we paint our nights with laughter, divine.

Embracing the Unseen

Your quirks are treasures I hold dear,
From the way you snort when you laugh sincere.
We embrace the odd, it's our favorite game,
Like socks without mates, never the same.

You juggle my heart while dropping my phone,
In this circus of love, I'm never alone.
With you by my side, every day is a ride,
Like a cat on a skateboard, we glide side by side.

You make faces that could stir a crowd,
With laughter that rolls, so boisterous and loud.
In shadows and light, our joy finds a way,
Together, we flutter like birds in a fray.

So here's to embracing the quirks that we share,
In this dance of the zany, we twirl without care.
With love that's a puzzle, we'll always be seen,
In this beautiful chaos, where we reign supreme.

Whispers of Forever

In the twilight, with stars all aglow,
We whisper sweet secrets, our private show.
I share my snacks, you give me a grin,
In this playful journey, we both win.

You tell me I'm weird, I just nod with cheer,
For in our oddness, we've crafted a sphere.
Like a clown at a party, I'm always amazed,
At how you find joy in the silliest ways.

Our laughter echoes, like bells in the night,
With mischief and joy, everything feels right.
From antics to whispers, we build our domain,
With love that's a riddle, it's never mundane.

So grab my hand and let's stroll 'til the dawn,
With laughter as fuel, we'll never move on.
As whispers of forever dance in our ears,
We'll cherish this laughter, through all of the years.

Tidal Waves of Affection

When I bring you lunch with my best dish,
You smile like it's the grandest wish.
But that soggy sandwich you'll never munch,
Still, you say it's sweet, and I feel the crunch.

On rainy days, we jump and splash,
Your giggles echo, oh what a clash!
My umbrella flips, we both look absurd,
Yet in that chaos, our joy's truly stirred.

In the kitchen, you dance like a star,
Tripping on noodles—you won't get far.
But you twirl and laugh, what a charming sight,
Even burnt toast can't dim your light.

So here's to our quirks, our silly old games,
Like two puzzle pieces, nobody claims.
With every wild moment, my heart takes flight,
In this quirky adventure, everything feels right.

As One We Rise

Together we tackle the forum of chores,
You vacuum my socks, while I lock the doors.
Your idea of dinner? A cereal mix,
Still, we laugh about it, no cause for conflicts.

When you wear my shirt, it's a fabulous sight,
Like a fashion show gone entirely right.
But my favorite part, oh can you guess?
Is how you strut, causing quite a mess!

In battles of wits, we're always in sync,
You paint your toenails while I try to think.
But your colorful toes spark a new debate,
Who knew foot fashion could rule our fate?

So cheers to the chaos we share every day,
In this whimsical life, come what may.
As one we rise, with laughter abound,
In the circus of love, we've truly been crowned.

Silhouettes of Serenity

Under the stars, we act like fools,
Dancing like penguins, breaking all rules.
Your moves so wacky, I can't help but snort,
While you claim it's ballet, oh what an export!

Candles are lit, but you trip on the cat,
Turning our dinner into a comical spat.
Yet, giggles emerge, like sparks flying high,
In our silly mishaps, we can't say goodbye.

Whispers at midnight, like secrets we share,
You speak of unicorns, which leads to despair.
But I smile and nod, just playing along,
In this silly duet, we can do no wrong.

So here's to the laughter, the joy that we find,
In moments like these, we're perfectly aligned.
For silhouettes of serenity won't wear us down,
In this circus of love, we wear the crown.

The Tides of Passion

You stole my fries and gave me a grin,
A criminal joy, oh where do I begin?
With ketchup on your nose, it's hard to stay mad,
In this playful ruckus, we're both just a tad.

At the movie night, we fight for the seat,
Popcorn on your lap, what a summer treat!
You choose the rom-com; I feign a big sigh,
But popcorn fights break out, oh my, oh my!

Silly bickering over who's the best cook,
You charred my cake; I just gave you a look.
Yet with sprinkles everywhere, we laugh and compare,
In this tasty debate, we're quite the pair.

So toast to our antics, our playful bliss,
In this tide of passion, it's hard to miss.
With each silly moment, our hearts intertwine,
In this joyful journey, forever you're mine.

Forever Ever After

In a land where socks go to hide,
We found each other, side by side.
You steal the fries, I take your drink,
Together we laugh, more than we think.

With silly jokes that never tire,
You set my heart, you light my fire.
We dance like fools in the rain,
Holding each other, crazy but sane.

Our quirks align like stars in the night,
You snore like a bear, but I hold you tight.
We share our dreams and sometimes our snacks,
In this game of love, there are no hacks.

For every mishap, there's a chuckle,
You trip on air, but it's worth the struggle.
With every giggle, we grow a bit fonder,
Forever together, our hearts will wander.

The Pulse Between Us

You say I'm nuts, I say you're sweet,
We dance through life on two left feet.
With every heartbeat, we find a way,
To make each moment a funny display.

You spill your coffee, I snort with glee,
Our love's a circus, just you and me.
With quirky puns and laughter loud,
We gather together, we form a crowd.

When life gives lemons, we make a pie,
With whipped cream laughs, we both can't deny.
Side by side, we tackle each game,
In each silly moment, we feel the flame.

So let's paint the world, in colors so bright,
With giggles and chaos that feels just right.
For in this pulse, we both can see,
The hilarity bound between you and me.

Beyond the Horizon

We set sail on a boat made of dreams,
Navigating life through giggles and screams.
You are the captain, I'm the first mate,
Together we sail, it's never too late.

The winds may blow, but we laugh in the face,
Of every wild wave that we bravely embrace.
With treasure maps full of quirky delights,
Finding gold dimes in the middle of nights.

Every sunset is like a slice of pie,
You know the secret – I'll never tell why.
We feast on our laughter, it's truly divine,
With crumbs of joy, we make the day shine.

Beyond the horizon, we'll find our way,
With silly adventures, come what may.
Through storms and sunshine, we'll always be,
Laughing together, it's you and me.

An Unbreakable Bond

We met at a party where no one would dance,
With a weird balloon, you took a wild chance.
You tripped on your feet, I laughed till I cried,
From that moment on, I knew we'd collide.

Your jokes are like magic, turning ice into flame,
Though sometimes your timing is truly to blame.
With playful nudges and glances so sly,
We turn the mundane into laughter-filled sky.

Through all of life's chaos, we'll stick like glue,
In a world of confusion, it's me and you.
With every new mishap, we share a grin,
An unbreakable bond formed deep within.

So here's to our journey, as lively as fun,
We'll keep laughing together till all's said and done.
For you are my partner, my anchor, my friend,
In this wild ride of life, laughter is the trend.

Elysium of Our Affection

In a world of quirky dreams,
We laugh at all our silly schemes,
You trip and spill your morning brew,
I just can't help but giggle too.

With each odd dance we try to pull,
You mock my moves, I take it cool,
Together we're a perfect pair,
Like socks that always find a chair.

Your jokes can sometimes make me cringe,
Yet I love you for each little binge,
Your laundry's mixed, it's true, I claim,
But you insist it's just our game.

In this space of pure delight,
We built our fortress, snug and tight,
Our world's a sitcom, full of cheer,
With you, I laugh from ear to ear.

Raindrops of Shared Joy

When the sky is dark and gray,
You bring a smile, come what may,
We splash around in puddles wide,
Like kids again, we take a ride.

Your quirky socks, a sight to see,
In mismatched patterns, wild and free,
We dance in storms, the laughter flows,
Underneath umbrellas, who knows?

With every drop, we sing our tune,
Two silly ducks, we chase the moon,
Your laughter rolls like thunder loud,
Together, we draw quite a crowd.

Through every storm, side by side,
Life's wild waves, we'll never hide,
In raindrops, joy is ours to blend,
A joyous chorus, on that we depend.

The Bridge of Unfaltering Hearts

Over rivers steep and wide,
We built a bridge, our love as guide,
With goofy antics and silly stunts,
We leap across, like playful fronts.

You say my jokes are quite a mess,
But with your grin, they're truly blessed,
Together we sway, we almost fall,
But laughter catches us through it all.

Like two lost cats in a sunbeam's glow,
We nap together, our mouths aglow,
In moments foolish, we find our spark,
With inside jokes that light the dark.

This bridge we cross, so smooth, so true,
With every giggle, I choose you,
In this madcap dance, we stand apart,
Yet together forever, heart to heart.

Dance of the Unbreakable

We sway like leaves in autumn air,
You twirl me round without a care,
Our feet, a tangle, oh what a sight,
With every move, we take to flight.

You're stepping left, I'm stepping right,
A duo of chaos, pure delight,
We bump and spin, oh what a spree,
Two giant clowns in harmony.

With a twist and shout, we trip a lot,
But I wouldn't change a single dot,
In this wild dance, our hearts collide,
Two silly souls, forever tied.

So grab my hand, let's take this chance,
In this bizarre waltz, we'll find romance,
An endless loop of giggly charms,
Forever safe in each other's arms.

The Strength of Tender Flames

Your snore is like a bear's growl,
But oh, how I still adore you now.
You spill the coffee, yet I pout,
In your clumsiness, there's never doubt.

We dance in socks on wooden floors,
Your spinning leads to laughter's roars.
You say you're lost, I simply grin,
Together, dear, we always win.

The laundry's mixed, your shirt is pink,
You shrug it off and start to wink.
The strength in us is oh-so-funny,
Your goofy ways are worth the honey.

So here's to us, a jolly pair,
With silly quirks beyond compare.
Through all the chaos, loud and bright,
In our warm chaos, love feels right.

Canvas of Our Dreams

In paint splatters, we find our way,
With you, my brush never goes astray.
You trip on hues, oh such a sight,
Yet in our mishaps, we paint delight.

Roses on walls, they look quite odd,
But in your eyes, they're like a god.
You drop the palette, laughter's bloom,
In every mess, we craft our room.

Our masterpieces are just for fun,
Doodles of joy, we come undone.
Through swirls and strokes, we laugh and scheme,
In every color, you are my dream.

So let's create this vivid show,
With wacky art that steals the glow.
In every splash, and every scream,
Together, dear, we're quite the team.

In the Arms of Forever

You steal the covers and take the bed,
Yet somehow, I'm not filled with dread.
In morning's light, with bedhead too,
    I still think it's a win with you.

Your socks are missing, now where'd they go?
A treasure hunt, with laughs on show.
Around the house, we search and seek,
    In silly games, we find our peak.

Dinner's burnt, oh, what a smell,
You crack a joke, and all is well.
With takeout menus at our side,
We feast on love, and you abide.

So here we sit, in cozy grace,
Each stumble brings a warm embrace.
In the arms of now, we never fret,
For this wild ride, I'll never regret.

The Unseen Thread

Through tangled cords, we find our way,
In every mishap, we dance and play.
You trip on words, I laugh aloud,
In your funny quirks, I'm always proud.

With mismatched shoes, we hit the street,
Your silly dance is quite the treat.
We chase the ice cream truck in glee,
A perfect world, just you and me.

You say you can't cook, I roll my eyes,
Yet burnt toast always wins the prize.
In every blunder, joy remains,
Our unbroken bond, it never wanes.

So here we are, tied side by side,
In laughter's grace, we take this ride.
Through every twist, we never dread,
With joys unseen, this thread we spread.

Through Life's Kaleidoscope

Through rainbows and laughter, we skip in the sun,
Chasing our shadows, oh, what silly fun!
With pie in our faces and shoes full of sand,
We dance like the dervishes, hand in hand.

Your snoring's my music, a lullaby sweet,
I trip on your socks as you dance on your feet.
With every misstep, a giggle erupts,
Together we stumble, oh, how we disrupt!

In markets we barter, I trade you a hug,
While you're busy negotiating, getting me snug.
With each silly wink and an eyebrow that's raised,
We turn every moment into a wild daze.

So let's play all day till the moon starts to glow,
With pancake wars nightly, we'll let the world know.
In our joyful circus, life spins with delight,
Forever you're mine in this quirky twilight.

A Dance of Destiny

Two left feet shuffle in the kitchen so bright,
You twirl and I spin, it's a comical sight.
The dog gives a howl, tries to join in the frolic,
As laughter erupts, nothing seems too symbolic.

With pizza in hand and sauce on our chin,
You wink and you grin, let the antics begin!
Our lives are a sitcom, each episode grand,
With pranks and with puns, as we walk hand in hand.

You hide little notes in my shoes and my coat,
Each one a reminder that life's a fun boat.
We've sailed through the chaos, embraced every quirk,
Finding joy in the mess, that's the work of our spark.

From costumes to karaoke, we take on the stage,
Our hearts beat in rhythm, let's turn a new page.
With every sweet moment, we dance through the night,
In this crazy adventure, we'll always be right!

Emblazoned in My Heart

You stole my fries, it's totally fair,
Your cheesy grin, beyond compare.
We laugh at moments, silly and bright,
In our own world, everything feels right.

Your snoring's loud, it scares the cat,
Yet here I am, still loving that.
You dance like no one's watching at all,
It's a wild sight, a hilarious ball.

Each quirky quirk, each funny face,
In this wacky love, I've found my place.
You're the punchline in my favorite joke,
Forever together, no need to provoke.

In sunshine or rain, with giggles we stand,
Hand in hand, making future plans.
I'll be your clown, your partner in crime,
In this bold story, we're lost in time.

Symphony of Two Souls

Your laugh is the tune that brings me delight,
A symphony played both day and night.
When you trip on air, it's pure comedy,
Dance like no one's watching, that's our melody.

Two hearts in rhythm, we'll never miss a beat,
You steal my popcorn, but it's a treat.
In our duet of chaos and dance,
I find my joy with just a glance.

With notes of laughter, we compose our song,
Together forever, where we both belong.
In this playful pit, we skip and sway,
Our laughter echoes, brightening the day.

So let's create beats that we can borrow,
In this funny dream, there's no room for sorrow.
Your silly quirks are music to my ears,
As we write our story, let's drown out our fears.

The Mountain of Our Togetherness

We climbed a hill, the view was grand,
I tripped and fell, right into the sand.
You laughed so hard, I thought you'd burst,
But that's the fun; I'm truly cursed!

Scaling life's heights, we zip and zoom,
With you, every stumble brings laughter in bloom.
You shout my name when I'm out of breath,
Yet together, we conquer even mischief and mess.

From dusk till dawn, through thick and thin,
Your wink ignites the mischief within.
Mountain high or valley low,
You're my perfect partner in every show.

Living each day as if it's a game,
No need for fortune; it's never the same.
In every tumble, in every cheer,
We'll stand hand in hand, no room for fear.

Pages of a Timeless Tale

In the book of us, it's quite absurd,
You snort when you laugh, it's the silliest word.
Each chapter unfolds with a twist of fate,
Our goofy love, it just can't wait.

We write our story with laughter and glee,
You steal my drink; you're so crafty!
From epic fails to breakfast in bed,
In this wacky life, we're joyfully led.

With sticky notes and sketches galore,
Your antics leave me begging for more.
A timeless tale that never grows old,
In pages of giggles, our dreams unfold.

So here's to us, to the chapters ahead,
With laughs and mishaps, we're easily led.
To every hiccup and every pun,
In the story of life, you're my favorite one.

Whispers of Eternal Embrace

In your hugs, I find my snack,
A hidden stash, I grab a pack.
Your laughter bounces off the walls,
Like rubber balls, it always calls.

When you snore, it's quite a show,
Your acrobatics steal the glow.
I try to leave, but hear a sound,
The pillow's pull keeps me around.

We dance like penguins on the floor,
Your two left feet make me adore.
In silly moments, we both dwell,
Like secret kids at the city well.

With you, my joy's a circus show,
A ticket stamped, I won't let go.
Your quirks are gems, all shiny bright,
Together, we'll be fools tonight!

In the Shadow of Your Heart

You steal my fries, my heart's delight,
The way you munch, it's quite a sight.
Your silly faces make me grin,
I might just let you have a win!

In the kitchen, you dance and sway,
Spilling flour on a sunny day.
With every slip, my laughter soars,
Who knew cooking could start a war?

You hum our song while doing chores,
A serenade that truly roars.
With dusters flying, who could fight?
Our messy love's a pure delight.

In shadows cast by goofy glee,
We make a mess, it's you and me.
With every tickle, hugs increase,
A silly waltz that won't cease!

Threads of Unbreakable Bond

Your puns are worse than dad's old jokes,
But I can't help but laugh, it pokes.
In tangled threads of wacky schemes,
We weave our lives in silly dreams.

The way you dance, all awkward grace,
Your feet stomp down, no need for space.
We leap like frogs in a silly spree,
To "Dancing Queen," it's you and me!

With toast that burns and coffee spills,
Our mornings glow with goofy thrills.
Each mishap makes our bond much strong,
In this wild life, we both belong.

So here's to us, the mismatched pair,
In laughter's thread, we breathe fresh air.
With goofy smiles, we take the chance,
To swirl through life in our strange dance!

Echoes of Us

In every echo, there's our song,
A silly verse, where we belong.
Your jokes may flop, but I don't mind,
In laughter's arms, our hearts entwined.

Through every stumble, giggles rise,
Your clumsy charm's a sweet surprise.
We chase each other round the park,
With shadows dancing in the dark.

From coffee spills to ice cream drips,
Life serves up all its little quips.
In every moment, we find the spark,
A playful light that leaves its mark.

So here we are, a pair so bright,
In echoes loud, we find our flight.
With every laugh, our spirits sing,
Together, we make the whole world swing!

Blooming in Each Other's Light

In the garden of our quirks,
You steal my fries, I steal your quirks.
We water laughter with crazy tales,
Planting smiles in whimsical trails.

Puns grow wild, a hybrid spree,
Your rhymes dance like bees in glee.
With each joke, the petals unfold,
In our patch, love's stories are bold.

Tickling fancies that bloom so bright,
Frolicking in the glow of night.
Your giggles echo like sweet perfume,
In this bouquet, our hearts zoom.

So here we stand, goofy and free,
In this garden, just you and me.
With every pun, a flower ignites,
Together we thrive in these silly delights.

Love's Uncharted Territory

We mapped our hearts like pirates, free,
On a treasure hunt for glee,
You brought the map, I brought snacks,
Navigating love with joy-filled hacks.

Our compass spins with playful glee,
As we dodge the storms of laundry spree.
Charting courses of ice cream cravings,
In our ship of dreams, the spirit raving.

X marks the spot for laughter's gold,
In uncharted lands, our stories unfold.
From pillow fights to silly debates,
In this treasure hunt, joy never waits.

So here's the deal, let's sail along,
In this voyage, we belong.
With every wave, our giggles rise,
In the sea of love, no goodbyes.

Radiance in Every Touch

When you tickle my side, it's a spark,
Like a match igniting in the dark.
Your hand in mine, electric delight,
Charging up laughter each silly night.

Every nudge is a dance, a chance,
To whirl in the chaos, join the prance.
You brush my shoulder, and I burst out,
With giggles and glee, that's what it's about.

In the rush of moments, we find our beat,
Like two left feet trying to meet.
With every poke, we bounce in place,
In our laughter, we find grace.

Together we glow, a comical spark,
Creating magic from the mundane dark.
In every touch, a radiant glow,
In quirky harmony, our spirits flow.

The Tapestry We Weave

Stitch by stitch, our laughter flows,
Creating patterns in every prose.
You quilt my heart with mischief's thread,
In this tapestry, joy's widespread.

Laughter weaves into every seam,
A fabric of antics, a vibrant dream.
I hold the colors, you bring the fun,
Interlaced moments, we're never done.

With each wacky thread, we embrace the jest,
In this quirky quilt, we find our best.
Your craziness pairs with my silliness,
A masterpiece born from our happiness.

So let's keep weaving this colorful tale,
Through ups and downs, we shall prevail.
In each patch, a memory thrives,
In this tapestry, our love survives.

The Depths of Devotion

I once bought you a goldfish,
To show my love, so you won't miss.
But it swam right out of its bowl,
Guess it took a solo stroll.

You laugh at my clumsy feet,
As I dance to our own beat.
With two left shoes, I twirl around,
Falling in love, on the ground.

At dinner, we both compete,
For the last of those tasty treats.
You overtook me with a grin,
And declared yourself the winner within.

Yet through it all, we don't mind,
Our silly ways are intertwined.
With giggles shared in every tune,
Our hearts just bounce like a cartoon.

Infinite Tides of Feeling

Remember when we lost our way,
In a sea of socks at the laundromat play?
You held one up, two colors mixed,
In a haze of laughter, our fates were fixed.

Your cooking skills? A comedy show,
With smoke alarms shouting to let you know.
Yet I dive into chaos, taste buds in flight,
Nourished by love, every day feels right.

At karaoke, you steal the mic,
With words so twisted, we laugh and bike.
The notes soar high, like kites in a breeze,
We sing out loud, trying hard to please.

Our love's a wave, washing ashore,
With every giggle, we ask for more.
In each splash, a joy that's unspoken,
In a world of jokes, we remain unbroken.

When Souls Collide

You tripped over my heart one day,
And now it's yours; what more can I say?
In awkward moments, we collide,
Like two ships sailing side by side.

With mismatched socks, we charm the crowd,
In our goofy ways, we stand out loud.
Our laughter echoes, the sound of glee,
As ants dance in your salad for free.

Let's host a picnic, with sandwiches bent,
An ant parade, as your task was spent.
You giggle and muse, 'Where did it go?'
My heart's in the sandwiches, you should know.

So here's our tale, absurd but bright,
Two silly souls, ever taking flight.
In the dance of life, we happily sway,
With grins that sparkle on the silliest day.

Anchored by Your Light

You shine like a beacon in my mind,
In a world of chaos, so hard to find.
With your goofy puns, and winks that sway,
You anchor my heart, come what may.

In our sock fort, we build our dreams,
With castles made of laughter, it seems.
We serve up snacks, a royal feast,
While the dog plots, aiming for a piece.

As we chase ducks at the local park,
You shout, 'I'm the ruler, hark!'
But they waddle away, no crown to wear,
And I laugh as you pretend to care.

Each day with you breaks the mundane,
In every slip, I feel no pain.
With you, I'm home, my guiding star,
An adventure absurd, wherever we are.

Chasing Forever

In a world where socks disappear,
We chase each other, oh so near.
With laughter bubbling, like soda pop,
Together we never, ever stop.

You say my dance moves are quite bizarre,
Yet I twirl like I'm a shining star.
We dodge the raindrops like it's a game,
Every slip and fall is just the same.

We build a fort from pillows high,
Pretending we're the kings on high.
In our kingdom, the snacks are grand,
With cookie shields, we take our stand.

So here we are, two goofy souls,
Sharing joy that endlessly rolls.
No need for crowns or fancy bling,
Just your grin makes my heart sing.

In the Embrace of Eternity

In a hug that seems to last all night,
Your breath, a tickle—it feels so right.
We giggle as we steal the sheets,
And dance like robots to silly beats.

Your morning hair—a wild beast,
Yet, to me, it is the greatest feast.
We'll conquer breakfast, toast in hand,
And laugh 'til we can hardly stand.

Through every mishap, we float like balloons,
Crafting chaos beneath the moon.
It's a circus when we share a meal,
With noodle fights that make us squeal.

Time fugitives, we fly and whirl,
In a world where you can't just twirl.
With every chuckle, every spin,
I find my forever tucked within.

Reflections in Each Other's Eyes

Your eyes are mirrors of comic grace,
Where silly faces find their place.
I see a dancer doing the cha-cha,
And just like that, we giggle 'ah-ha!'

You claim you can't sing a single note,
Yet serenades are in every quote.
With off-key melodies, we wildly sway,
And laugh as neighbors call it a day.

Our reflections splash across the park,
Chasing ducks while we leave a mark.
We paint the world with splashes bright,
With raucous joy from day to night.

In the funniest of moments, we see,
The depth of love in our giant glee.
A play of smiles, a jolly surprise,
In this dance, I see in your eyes.

The Depth of Us

Beneath the wit, there lies a spark,
Where jests and puns leave their mark.
Like two old socks without a match,
Finding humor, what a perfect catch.

Our plans may flop, and dinner too,
Yet together, we always make do.
From burnt toast to a giggle fit,
You and I, forever, we won't quit.

In wild adventures and pizza fights,
We embrace the chaos of those nights.
With every blunder, stronger we grow,
In the depths of laughter, our love glows.

So here's to us, the perfectly strange,
In this crazy life, we won't change.
With moments messy, bright, and fun,
Together, we're the perfect pun.

Lanterns in Shared Darkness

In a world where spoons are forks,
We dance between the silly sparks.
Your laughter lights the gloomy night,
With you, my heart takes flight.

We trip on dreams and play charades,
With every silly game we've made.
You steal my fries and claim a bite,
But I don't mind, it feels so right.

We wear our quirks like cozy hats,
Like dancing cats and silly chats.
With lanterns bright, we chase the night,
In shared darkness, your smile's the light.

So here's to us, the jesters bold,
With every story, love unfolds.
In our own circus, life's a song,
With laughter sweet, we can't go wrong.

Visions of Endless Togetherness

In the kitchen, cooking's a feat,
You burn the toast, yet it's a treat.
I'll make the coffee, oh what fun,
You spill it all, still number one.

We plot and plan our wild escape,
With pizza boxes, we'll shape a cape.
Two superheroes, side by side,
Exploring life as our fun ride.

Your quirky dance, my goofy sway,
In every moment, we find a way.
We'll paint the walls with laughter bright,
In visions clear, our hearts ignite.

Together we're a wacky team,
Chasing dreams like wild ice cream.
Oh how I cherish every day,
With you, my world's a cabaret.

Boundless Hearts

Our love's a ride on roller coasters,
Screaming loud like silly jokesters.
With every twist, my heart skips beats,
Your laughter's my favorite treat.

We'll chase the ducks and watch them waddle,
In life's grand boat, we're made to paddle.
The world is big, yet small we roam,
With every silly step, it feels like home.

You wear my hat, I wear your shoes,
In this big game, we cannot lose.
Our hearts bound tight like silly string,
In this crazy life, together we sing.

Through all the mess, I can't complain,
Your quirks and laughs keep me sane.
With boundless hearts, we'll play our part,
In each other's dreams, we'll never part.

Through the Veil of Time

In our own time machine, we glide,
With every hour, we laugh and bide.
Through ancient tales, we spin and twirl,
In every moment, our flags unfurl.

We dance on clouds, we jump through hoops,
Like two lost souls in silly loops.
With snacks in hand, we conquer the night,
Through space and time, we make it right.

Your jokes are cheesy, your puns absurd,
But laughter's magic, it's never blurred.
We'll steal the sun, ignite the sky,
With every glance, we're flying high.

So let's create our stories bold,
With every adventure, love unfolds.
Through the veil of time, we roam hand in hand,
In this wild journey, together we stand.

Starlit Promises

Under the moon, we dance quite rare,
Your two left feet, I can't help but stare.
With every twirl, we trip and fall,
Together we laugh, it's the best of all.

We promised the stars a silly routine,
But your clumsy charm is always so keen.
With every antics, my heart does sing,
Oh, what joy your laughter can bring.

In a world of chaos, you're my sweet jest,
Our quirks are the gems, we treasure the best.
Like socks on a cat, we shimmy and slide,
With you by my side, there's nowhere to hide.

So let's chase the silly, the fun yet untold,
In our starlit promises, never grow old.
With giggles and whispers, we'll sway through the night,
Just you and me, oh what a delightful sight.

Everlasting Whispers

In the hush of the night, your snoring's a song,
A melody sweet, though it's far from strong.
I whisper soft secrets while you steal the sheets,
Each breath a reminder, oh, the love that repeats.

Your hair's a disaster, like a bird's nest alive,
But your goofy grin makes my heart dive.
We share little jokes that only we know,
In our quiet moments, happiness flows.

From tickles and giggles to playful little fights,
You're my silly partner, my joy and my light.
With every shared glance, the world fades away,
Whispers of laughter, that's how we play.

So let's keep it goofy, forever and more,
In our everlasting whispers, there's always a score.
With you as my comic, my heart will remain,
In this wacky dance, life's never mundane.

Vows Written in the Stars

We wrote our vows on a back of a napkin,
Over spilled coffee, oh what a captain!
"Forever and ever," you boldly declared,
But forgot the ketchup—you were so unprepared.

With laughter that echoes through thick and thin,
You swear it's my fault when you don't win.
But I know the secrets that make our hearts race,
Through silly debates, we found our own space.

We dance through the aisles of our wacky delight,
Where frozen pizza counts as gourmet tonight.
With vows that may wobble and twist in the breeze,
We conquer each moment, our clumsiness frees.

So raise up a toast to the fun and the wild,
To vows scribbled hastily, yet tender and mild.
In this charming chaos, our hearts are a blaze,
Written in starlight, forever we'll graze.

The Essence of You and Me

Your socks are unmatched, just like your style,
But they make me chuckle, they always beguile.
From breakfast in bed to burnt toast galore,
You're the spice in my life, who could ask for more?

We duel with our puns and giggle all day,
Turning mundane tasks into comedic play.
Your quirks are the treasures that brighten my scene,
Like mismatched shoes sprucing up my routine.

We chase down the laughter, from dawn until dusk,
In this tangle of chaos, there's always a trust.
Like bubbles in soda, we fizz and we pop,
With you, my dear darling, the fun never stops.

So here's to our journey, the wacky embrace,
In the essence of you and me, we've found our place.
With humor our banner, we'll laugh through it all,
In this grand adventure, together we'll sprawl.

Illuminated Pathways

In the glow of your smile, I trip and I fall,
Banana peels near, you giggle, enthrall.
Your laughter's a beacon, leading me right,
Together we wander, hearts light as a kite.

Your socks mismatched, a fashion faux pas,
Yet in my eyes, you shine like a star.
We dance in the kitchen, chopsticks in hand,
Stirring up chaos, the best kind of jam.

Every hiccup and snort, an echoing tune,
Our clumsy ballet beneath the full moon.
With pizza in one hand, and love in the other,
You're my culinary partner, brother and mother.

In your quirky charm, I lose and I find,
Laughter flutters softly, like butterflies blind.
As we leap through the puddles, with socks full of glee,
This silly adventure, forever with thee.

Resonance of the Heart

Your snore is a symphony, a loud serenade,
In dreams I'm the hero, out on parade.
We wrestle for covers; it's a nightly fight,
A cuddle, a grumble, then all feels just right.

With cereal tossed and milk clouds galore,
You make breakfast messy, who could ask for more?
Your wink turns the morning into a light show,
Even coffee spills seem to steal the show.

We race for the last cupcake, fists full of cream,
Your frosting-topped victory is cruel, so it seems.
Yet every sweet battle brings giggles anew,
In this wild pastry war, I'm always for you.

In each whispered pun, in each playful jest,
Together we laugh; it's simply the best.
Our hearts beat in riddle, each note a delight,
In the rhythm we forge, everything feels right.

Gateways to Forever

Lost in your antics, we chase after fun,
With silly string rockets and gooey gum.
Each prank turns to giggles, a chorus of joy,
As we dance in the kitchen, two kids with a toy.

The cat gives a glare; our circus unfolds,
We slide on the floor, brave, reckless, bold.
With lemonade arches and popcorn galore,
A carnival's magic, we endlessly score.

Oh, the sock puppet show with voices galore,
You laugh so hard, you can't take it anymore.
With jello shots bouncing, a wiggle, a shake,
We're the clowns in this story, make no mistake.

Through each wild adventure, I know we will roam,
Building our laughter, we've found a new home.
In each playful tale, there's a map we've drawn,
Gateways to forever, from dusk until dawn.

A Symphony Unbroken

You sing in the shower, a Broadway debut,
Off-key but with flair, each note rings so true.
I join in your chorus, the dog gives a bark,
A duet that echoes, brightening the dark.

Board games are battles, with laughter and sighs,
You cheat with a wink, those mischievous eyes.
Yet, rolling the dice always leads to more fun,
The king and the queen of this game we have spun.

We hold epic dance-offs, silly and free,
In a living room jungle, just you and me.
A mix of wild moves, 'til the neighbors complain,
But we just keep grooving, there's so much to gain.

With jokes on the tip of our tongue every day,
Our world spins in circles, but we're here to stay.
In this symphony audio, sweet music we make,
With laughter in tandem, we never will break.

www.ingramcontent.com/pod-product-compliance
Ingram Content Group UK Ltd.
Pitfield, Milton Keynes, MK11 3LW, UK
UKHW020102171224
452675UK00013B/1277